**Lo Linkert: Hunters
Fishermen
and other
Liars**

HUNTERS FISHERMEN
and other
LIARS

PLAINSMAN PUBLICATIONS LTD.

Published and distributed in Canada by
Plainsman Publications Ltd.
2133 Quebec Street
Vancouver, B.C. V5T 2Z9

Simultaneously published in the U.S. by
Jolex Inc., Oakland, New Jersey and
distributed by John Olson Company
294 West Oakland Avenue
Oakland, New Jersey 07436

Vertrieb für Europa:
Journal-Verlag Schwend GmbH
Schwaebisch Hall, W. Germany

Printed in the U.S.A.
ISBN: 0-89149-060-4

First printing: 1979
Second printing: 1980

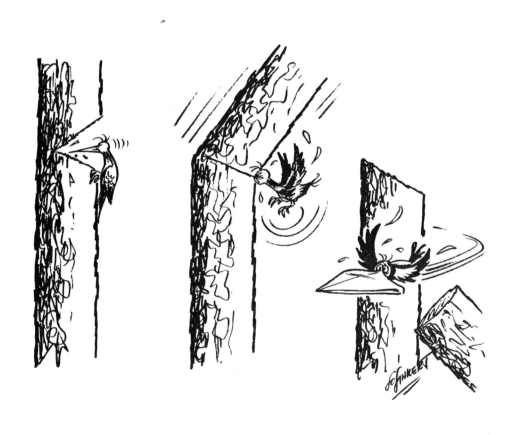

"BLESS YOU!"

"BAIT? WHAT'S BAIT?"

"IF IT'S A SCHOOL WE'RE CERTAINLY
TEACHING THEM A LESSON!"

"GEZUNDHEIT!"

"SORRY, HERB, BUT WE'RE ALL FILLED UP!"

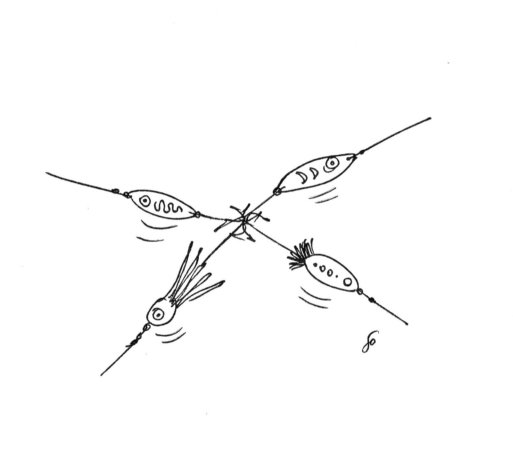

"FIVE YEARS!.....OR TELL ME WHERE YOU CAUGHT HIM!"

HURRY UP! I WANT TO KNOW IF I'M PATIENT ENOUGH TO FISH.

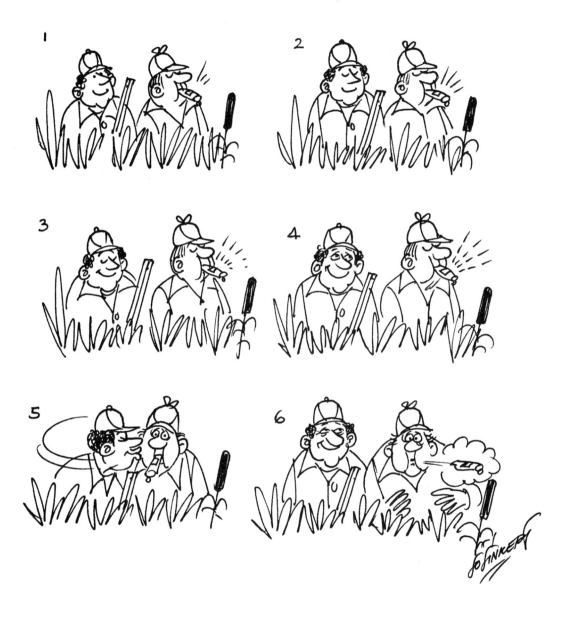

"LET'S GET HER DOWN AND DO SOME FISHING!"

"THEY MUST BE AFTER SARDINES!"

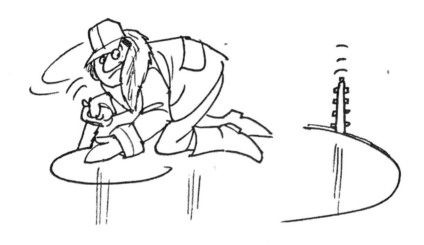

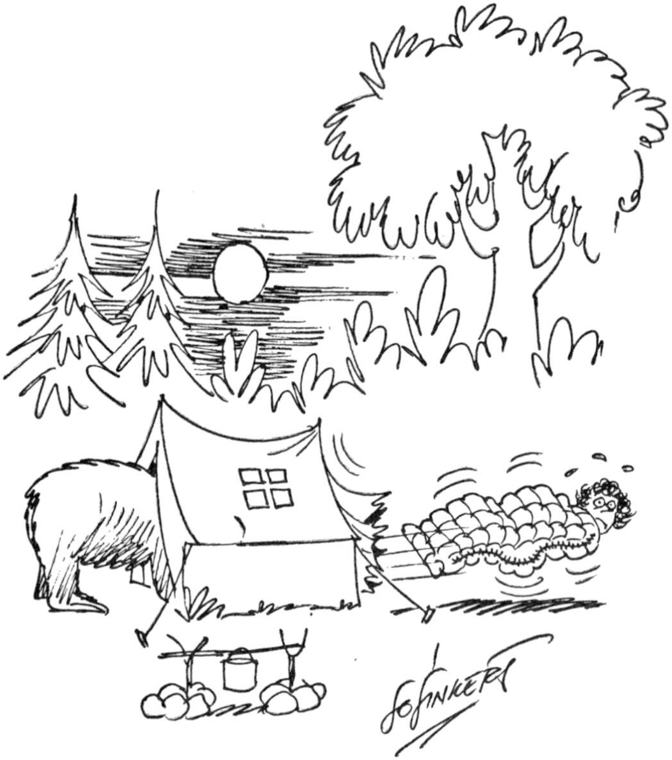

"CHICKEN!"

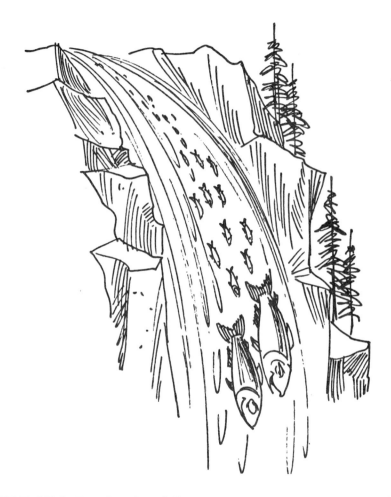

"THAT WAS FUN! LET'S TRY IT AGAIN SOMETIME!"

"THOSE THINGS MUST COST THEM A FORTUNE!"

"GO BACK TO SLEEP, DUMDUM......
IT'S ONLY HALF PAST DECEMBER! "

"HARRY, THIS WORM REFUSES
TO BITE INTO THE HOOK! "

"GIVE HIM MORE LINE, HENRY!"

"HOW LONG DO YOU WANT ME TO MAKE THIS WORM, DAD?"

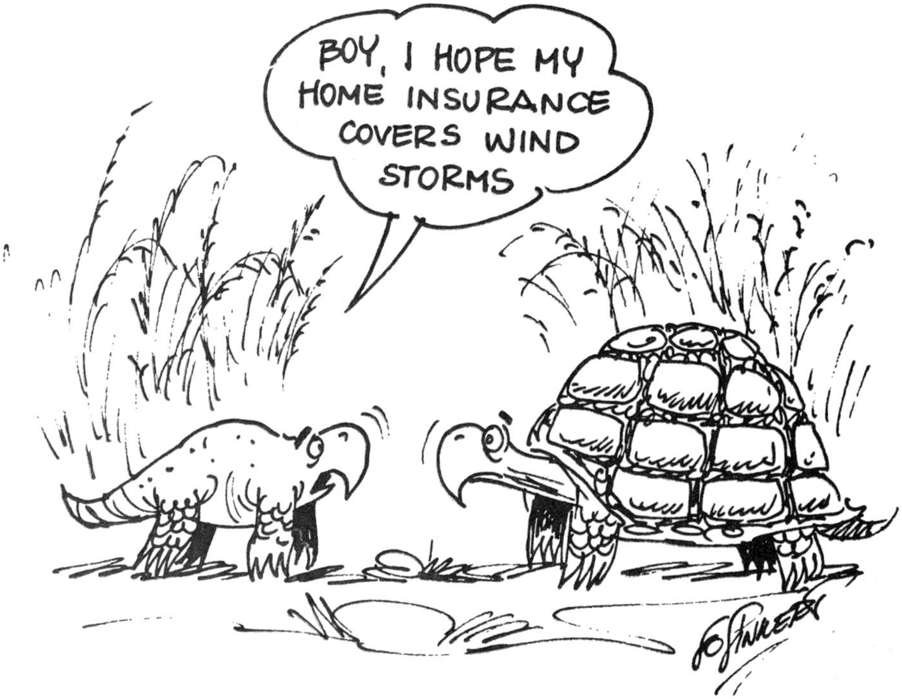
BOY, I HOPE MY HOME INSURANCE COVERS WIND STORMS

"OKAY, I KILLED HIM....YOU CLEAN HIM!"

"WHO INVITED HIM?"

Lo Linkert CARTOON SERIES

Golftoons

For Golftoons, Lo has selected his best golf cartoons, placing them under one cover. His hilarious talking golf ball is liberally sprinkled throughout the text. Lo's best barbs, however, are directed towards the frustrated duffer who suffers momentary lapses in etiquette. This is a book that every golfer will enjoy — on the 19th hole, in the locker room, or in the comfort of an easy chair by the fire.

Laugh Off the Pounds

After years of listening to friends talking about their diets, Lo has come up with his own weight-loss method — a diet of laughter.

Cointoons

Cartoons with dollars, francs, kroners and pfennigs are no easy task, but Lo has come up with some first-class humor.

Also by Lo Linkert:
**Stamptoons (German only)
Golftoons Calendar
Golftoons Posters**

Look for these items in your bookstore or write to the publisher, **Plainsman Publications Ltd., 2133 Quebec St., Vancouver, B.C., Canada V5T 2Z9.**

In the United States:
**The John Olson Company
294 West Oakland Avenue
Oakland, New Jersey 07436**